WRITE ✓ START
WRITING PROMPTS WITH RUBRICS

WORDS TO WRITE

Mary K. Cassaday

JAMESTOWN ⛵ PUBLISHERS
a division of NTC/CONTEMPORARY PUBLISHING GROUP
Lincolnwood, Illinois USA

This vocabulary prompt book was designed for the middle-school classroom. It contains words suitable for grades five through eight. The format of the book lends itself to a word a day during one semester of classes. Although exercises are provided for each word, they may be used merely as a springboard for your own ideas. We hope you will find the book beneficial for your students to use in both writing and speaking.

ISBN: 0-89061-083-5

Published by Jamestown Publishers,
a division of NTC/Contemporary Publishing Group, Inc.
4255 West Touhy Avenue
Lincolnwood (Chicago), Illinois 60646-1975, U.S.A.

Manufactured in the United States of America

890 ML 0 9 8 7 6 5 4 3 2 1

Contents

Abdomen

Definition The part of the body between the chest and the hips

Example Mark went to the doctor after bending double from the pain in his **abdomen**.

Respond

A pain in the **abdomen** can be something simple or something serious. What do you think Mark's **abdominal** problem is? Will he be all right? Finish the story.

_____

_____

_____

_____

_____

_____

_____

_____

_____

_____

_____

_____

_____

_____

Abolish

Definition   To do away with

Example   The student council did not want to **abolish** the dress code.

Respond

It's a new year and you're a candidate for the student council. Select something else the student body does not want to see **abolished** and plan how to use it in your campaign. Defend your position on the **abolishment** of this item.

_____

_____

_____

_____

_____

_____

_____

_____

_____

_____

_____

_____

_____

_____

_____

_____

_____

_____

Absentee

Definition   Having to do with a person who is not present

Example   People who are unable to get home on Election Day often vote by **absentee** ballot.

Respond

When you don't go to school you are an **absentee** that day. What are some of the things that might occur if the school had too many **absentees**?

_____

_____

_____

_____

_____

_____

_____

_____

_____

_____

_____

_____

_____

_____

_____

Advertisement

Definition   A paid public announcement

Example   The newspaper **advertisement** guaranteed "Prices that won't ruffle your feathers."

Respond

Advertisements are designed to sell products. Therefore those that attract attention are more likely to be successful. If you had a product to sell, would your **advertisement** be on radio, on television, or in newspapers? Which would be the most effective place to spend your **advertising** money and why?

_____

_____

_____

_____

_____

_____

_____

_____

_____

_____

_____

_____

_____

_____

_____

Ambition

Definition   The desire for success

Example   Tyrone's greatest **ambition** in life is to be a judge.

Respond

Ambition is something everyone possesses. Some just have more than others. What is your greatest **ambition**? Have you made a plan to attain it and what do you think the outcome will be?

_____
_____
_____
_____
_____
_____
_____
_____
_____
_____
_____
_____
_____
_____
_____
_____
_____

Amuse

Definition   To entertain; to keep busy with an enjoyable activity

Example   Scott was bored. He wanted something to **amuse** himself. He could play basketball or tennis, or he could go FISHING! Fishing was the best **amusement** of all.

Respond

What **amuses** you the most? a game? a person? a place? Why does this particular thing **amuse** you?

_____

_____

_____

_____

_____

_____

_____

_____

_____

_____

_____

_____

_____

_____

_____

_____

Anxious

Definition   Eager

Example   Sarah was so **anxious** to get to the mall that she forgot her purse.

Respond

A person who is **anxious** to do something is sometimes called an "eager beaver." Maybe this describes you when you are **anxious** to go somewhere. Think of a time in your past when something funny or strange happened because you were **anxious**.

_____

_____

_____

_____

_____

_____

_____

_____

_____

_____

_____

_____

_____

_____

_____

_____

Astronomy

Definition   The science that deals with the sun, moon, stars, and planets

Example   **Astronomy** is one of the oldest sciences.

Respond

Many careers are available for **astronomers**. They may teach, conduct research, help plan space explorations, and assist in developing equipment for spacecraft. **Astronomers** need many different skills. You are planning a career in **astronomy**. Make an educational plan containing the courses you feel you should take in preparation for this career.

_____

_____

_____

_____

_____

_____

_____

_____

_____

_____

_____

_____

_____

Avenge

Definition   To get even for an injury or a wrong

Example   Our team wanted to **avenge** the loss to the Tigers by winning their next game.

Respond

Some people spend their entire lives trying to **avenge** one thing or another. What do you think the world would be like if everyone spent their lives seeking **vengeance**?

_____

_____

_____

_____

_____

_____

_____

_____

_____

_____

_____

_____

_____

_____

_____

_____

_____

_____

_____

Balk

Definition   To stubbornly refuse to move
or act

Example   As the mules were led toward the
barn, suddenly one of them
began to **balk**. Jonah pulled and
tugged, but the mule just **balked**
even more.

Respond

Pretend you are Jonah. How might you get the **balking** mule to go into the barn?

_____

_____

_____

_____

_____

_____

_____

_____

_____

_____

_____

_____

_____

_____

_____

_____

Blackmail

Definition   Forcing someone to do or pay something by the use of threats

Example   "**Blackmail** is a crime," yelled Tom to the man on the phone.
"Pay up or I'll tell your secret," replied the evil **blackmailer**.

Respond

Tom was frightened. He didn't know how to deal with **blackmail**. He didn't want his secret told but he couldn't afford what the **blackmailer** wanted. From the lead given, finish the story. What was Tom's secret? How much was the **blackmailer** asking for?

_____

_____

_____

_____

_____

_____

_____

_____

_____

_____

_____

_____

_____

Bookworm

Definition   A person who is very fond of
reading and studying

Example   Sharon called Susan a **bookworm,**
and it made her cry.

Respond

Sometimes a person who makes very good grades is called a **bookworm**.
This is very unfair because being a **bookworm** is just as good as being
an athlete. What would you do if someone called you a **bookworm**?
Would you just stop studying? What would happen if you did?

_____

_____

_____

_____

_____

_____

_____

_____

_____

_____

_____

_____

_____

_____

_____

_____

_____

Calculate

Definition   To find out by computing; to use arithmetic

Example   Bill wanted to **calculate** his grade average in health class. He discovered that his **calculations** were not even close to what he thought his average should be.

Respond

Calculating averages is often called for in solving math problems. Explain how you would **calculate** your grade average.

_____

_____

_____

_____

_____

_____

_____

_____

_____

_____

_____

_____

_____

_____

_____

_____

_____

_____

Capable

Definition Able to do something well

Example Mrs. Perkins is known as a very **capable** teacher.

Respond

When a person is described as being **capable**, it usually means that he or she is doing a very good job. If you were in charge of the school dance and you wanted the most **capable** person to do the decorations, how would you make the selection?

_____
_____
_____
_____
_____
_____
_____
_____
_____
_____
_____
_____
_____
_____
_____
_____

14

Captivity

Definition The condition of being held against one's will

Example During the Vietnam War, many American soldiers were held in **captivity**.

Respond

No one wants to be held in **captivity**. What do you think the feelings would be of someone who is being held in **captivity**?

_____
_____
_____
_____
_____
_____
_____
_____
_____
_____
_____
_____
_____
_____
_____
_____
_____

Caravan

Definition   A group—such as merchants, pilgrims, or tourists—traveling together

Example   The ball players, cheerleaders, and fans formed a **caravan** to go to the state tournament.

Respond

Caravans were once formed for the purpose of safety, but today they're formed for fun. Have you ever traveled anywhere in a **caravan**? Discuss the advantages and disadvantages of traveling in a **caravan**.

_____

_____

_____

_____

_____

_____

_____

_____

_____

_____

_____

_____

_____

_____

Collision

Definition   The act of hitting or striking
             violently together

Example   The head-on **collision** left
             the two cars badly damaged.

Respond

It is not necessary for both objects to be moving in order to have a **collision**.
You might be running and **collide** with a wall or a fence or some other object.
Have you ever seen a **collision** of any kind? If so, what was it and what was
the outcome?

_____

_____

_____

_____

_____

_____

_____

_____

_____

_____

_____

_____

_____

_____

_____

_____

Combine

Definition   To join; to bring together

Example   The great cooks of the world work many hours to **combine** different foods to create new and exciting dishes.

Respond

It's Daddy's turn to cook and he needs your help. Plan a meal **combining** foods that will go well together and explain the **combination** to your father.

_____
_____
_____
_____
_____
_____
_____
_____
_____
_____
_____
_____
_____
_____
_____
_____
_____
_____

Consult

Definition   To seek advice

Example   Jason decided he should **consult** his
doctor for the pain in his head before
taking any aspirin.

Respond

Very often people need to **consult** someone who knows more
about a situation than they do. When might you need to
consult someone to help you solve a problem? Who are
some of the people you might **consult**?

_____

_____

_____

_____

_____

_____

_____

_____

_____

_____

_____

_____

_____

_____

_____

_____

_____

Counterfeit

Definition   False; not real

Example   The funny-looking little man entered the bank and said, "Stick 'em up!" As everyone raised their hands, he spotted a large bag of money sitting a few feet away. He grabbed the bag and ran out the door, thinking he had struck it rich. He was soon to realize how wrong he was, because the bag was full of **counterfeit** money.

Respond

Sometimes people are fooled by something that is **counterfeit**. In a short story, tell about a time when someone was fooled by an object or feeling that was **counterfeit**.

_____

_____

_____

_____

_____

_____

_____

_____

_____

_____

_____

_____

_____

_____

Daze

Definition A state of bewilderment or surprise

Example Luke sat in a **daze** after hearing he had won the state lottery.

Respond

What will happen when Luke comes out of his **daze**? Will he be happy that he has won? Will he be too **dazed** to use his money wisely? What will his future be like?

_____

_____

_____

_____

_____

_____

_____

_____

_____

_____

_____

_____

_____

_____

_____

_____

_____

Name _____ Date _____

Demanding

Definition   Requiring much effort or attention

Example   Mr. Meany was a very **demanding** boss.

Respond

Mr. Meany expected everyone to work long, hard hours. He **demanded** that the employees forget about themselves and their families while they were at work. Pretend that you are one of Mr. Meany's employees. Predict what will happen if someone in your family becomes ill and needs you and you don't meet Mr. Meany's **demands**.

_____

_____

_____

_____

_____

_____

_____

_____

_____

_____

_____

_____

_____

_____

_____

22

Deplane

Definition   To get out of an airplane after landing

Example   The flight attendant asked the passengers to **deplane** in an orderly manner.

Respond

Have you ever flown in an airplane? Were you given any special instructions for **deplaning**? Perhaps if you haven't flown you may have seen movies about airplanes. If so, did anything unusual happen while the passengers were **deplaning**? What was the outcome? Did all go well? Complete a story about **deplaning**.

_____

_____

_____

_____

_____

_____

_____

_____

_____

_____

_____

_____

_____

_____

_____

Derby

Definition A type of hat; a type of horse race

Example Sam wore a **derby** when he watched the Kentucky **Derby**.

Respond

Some words, such as **derby**, have two totally different meanings. Choose one meaning and tell a story about a **derby**.

_____
_____
_____
_____
_____
_____
_____
_____
_____
_____
_____
_____
_____
_____
_____
_____
_____
_____

Dormitory

Definition   A building with many sleeping rooms

Example   Levi and Omar plan to live together in
a **dormitory** when they go to college.

Respond

Dormitory life is one of the most exciting experiences of attending college.
Lifelong friendships begin in **dormitories**. Do you plan to live in a **dormitory**
when you go to college? What kind of roommate do you hope to have?

_____

_____

_____

_____

_____

_____

_____

_____

_____

_____

_____

_____

_____

_____

_____

Dramatize

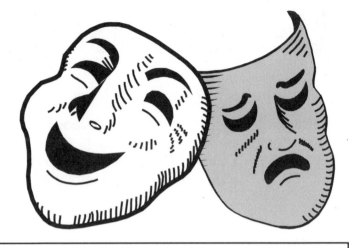

Definition   To make something seem tense or exciting

Example   Jason asked Sandra, "Please don't **dramatize** every story you tell."

Respond

Sometimes individuals are called **dramatic** because they tend to **dramatize** everything. Does it make a story more interesting if the teller **dramatizes** it? Describe someone you know who tends to **dramatize**.

_____

_____

_____

_____

_____

_____

_____

_____

_____

_____

_____

_____

_____

_____

_____

_____

Easel

Definition   The stand that holds an artist's pictures

Example   Ramon stood at his **easel** for hours, painting beautiful scenes.

Respond

Everyone can't paint the scenes they find beautiful, but everyone can appreciate them. What would be in the pictures on your **easel** if you were an artist?

_____

_____

_____

_____

_____

_____

_____

_____

_____

_____

_____

_____

_____

_____

_____

_____

Elicit

Definition   To call forth; to bring out

Example   The teacher was trying very hard to **elicit**
a response from his students.

Respond

Eliciting a response from students usually isn't a problem, because it seems
that most of them want to talk all the time. There are times, though, when
students are reluctant to answer. Why do you hesitate when the teacher tries
to **elicit** a response?

_____

_____

_____

_____

_____

_____

_____

_____

_____

_____

_____

_____

_____

_____

_____

_____

_____

Exile

Definition   A period of forced absence from one's country
or home

Example   Napoleon's **exile** to Elba lasted less than a year.

Respond

Exile was once used as a form of punishment for certain crimes.
Exile is still used in some cultures. Do you think **exile** is a fair
punishment? Why or why not?

_____

_____

_____

_____

_____

_____

_____

_____

_____

_____

_____

_____

_____

_____

_____

_____

Expand

Definition   To become larger

Example   The children watched in
awe as the air blown into
the beautiful balloons
caused them to **expand**.

Respond

If you were **expanding** balloons with air, how would you know how much air
you could put in before it became too much? What happens if you **expand**
the balloons too much? Would the same thing happen if you **expanded** a
tire too much?

_____

_____

_____

_____

_____

_____

_____

_____

_____

_____

_____

_____

_____

_____

Name _____ Date _____

Foresight

Definition   Careful thought for the future

Example   Charles had the **foresight** to begin
planning his future long before he
graduated from high school.

Respond

Have you ever heard the expression, "Hindsight is twenty-twenty"?
Foresight can also be twenty-twenty. Using your **foresight**, where do
you picture yourself in ten years?

_____

_____

_____

_____

_____

_____

_____

_____

_____

_____

_____

_____

_____

_____

_____

Fragile

Definition   Easily damaged or broken

Example   The beautiful china cup was so **fragile** that Emily was almost afraid to pick it up.

Respond

Feelings are also very **fragile**. What hurts your feelings? Have you done things to hurt other's feelings? Is there someone you have to handle **fragilely** in order not to hurt their feelings?

_____

_____

_____

_____

_____

_____

_____

_____

_____

_____

_____

_____

_____

_____

_____

_____

Furious

Definition Full of anger

Example Jennifer was **furious** with her friend Mona because Mona had sent a Valentine card to John. Little did she know that Mona was just as **furious** because Jennifer had sent a card to David.

Respond

Many times someone becomes **furious** with a friend because of a very small problem. Has this ever happened to you? Were you really, really **furious** and how did you work out the problem?

_____

_____

_____

_____

_____

_____

_____

_____

_____

_____

_____

_____

_____

_____

_____

Gallant

Definition   Brave and noble; courteous and attentive to women

Example   Sir Walter Raleigh was called a **gallant** man because he spread his coat over a mud puddle for the queen to walk on.

Respond

Acts of **gallantry** have been cited throughout history. However, **gallant** is a word we seldom hear today. Give an example and explain what you consider to be a **gallant** act.

_____

_____

_____

_____

_____

_____

_____

_____

_____

_____

_____

_____

_____

_____

_____

_____

Grief

Definition   Deep sorrow

Example   Gabriella shared Diego's **grief** over the loss of his dog.

Respond

Grief is an emotion that all of us share. It may come from the loss of a pet, a friend, or a family member. What loss in your life has caused you the most **grief**? Who shared your **grief** with you?

_____

_____

_____

_____

_____

_____

_____

_____

_____

_____

_____

_____

_____

_____

_____

_____

Henceforth

Definition   From now on

Example   "**Henceforth** you will have your
                 homework ready on time or
                 you will stay after school,"
                 thundered Mr. Sanchez.

Respond

"**Henceforth**," thought Jimmy to himself. "What in the world does that mean?"
How should Jimmy find out what **henceforth** means? Once he finds out,
he will have added a new word to his vocabulary. Make a list of things
you resolve **henceforth** never to do.

_____

_____

_____

_____

_____

_____

_____

_____

_____

_____

_____

_____

_____

_____

_____

_____

Name _____ Date _____

Hibernate

Definition   To spend the winter in sleep

Example   The grizzly bear searched for a cave in which to **hibernate**.

Respond

Bears are not the only animals who **hibernate** during the winter. Even humans sometimes feel the urge to sleep away a few days. Have you ever told a friend that you were going to **hibernate** during a cold, rainy weekend? Did you do it? How did it turn out?

_____

_____

_____

_____

_____

_____

_____

_____

_____

_____

_____

_____

_____

_____

Illustrate

Definition To make clear or explain by stories, pictures, examples, or comparisons

Example Rosa drew beautiful pictures to **illustrate** the story Carmen had written.

Respond

Everyone can think of at least one book that was much more interesting because it was **illustrated** so well. What other examples of **illustrations** can you think of and why are they important?

_____

_____

_____

_____

_____

_____

_____

_____

_____

_____

_____

_____

_____

_____

_____

Immigrant

Definition   A person who comes into a foreign
country or region to live

Example   For many years Ellis Island was the
port of entry for any **immigrant**
who came to New York City.

Respond

The United States has often been called the "melting pot"
because of the many different countries its **immigrants**
have come from. Your family may be descended from
immigrants from more than one country. Based on what
you know of your family history, decide what countries the
immigrants in your family came from.

_____

_____

_____

_____

_____

_____

_____

_____

_____

_____

_____

_____

Independence

Definition   Freedom from the control of others

Example   America declared its **independence** on July 4, 1776.

Respond

America spent many years under British rule before attaining her **independence**. Other countries have also had to fight for their **independence**, but many have not handled it as well as our nation did. Have you studied about another country that gained its **independence** only to lose it because the people didn't know how to live **independently**? What might they have done differently?

_____

_____

_____

_____

_____

_____

_____

_____

_____

_____

_____

_____

_____

_____

_____

_____

Indulgent

Definition   Too kind or agreeable; giving in to another's desires

Example   Frank soon learned that his mother was so **indulgent** he could get anything he wanted by having a temper tantrum.

Respond

Parents don't always do their children a favor by being too **indulgent**. Have you ever known someone whose parents were very **indulgent**? Were they right, and why do you think so?

_____

_____

_____

_____

_____

_____

_____

_____

_____

_____

_____

_____

_____

_____

_____

_____

_____

Insect

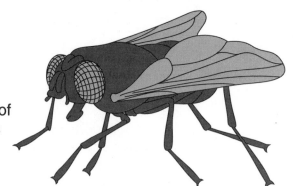

Definition   Any of a group of small, spineless
animals with the body divided into
three parts and having three pairs of
legs and usually two pairs of wings

Example   Houseflies and crickets are two
common forms of **insects**.

Respond

Akira was dreaming that a giant **insect** was trying to get into his room.
Tell a story about **insects** by completing Akira's dream.

_____

_____

_____

_____

_____

_____

_____

_____

_____

_____

_____

_____

_____

_____

_____

_____

Interior

Definition   The inside or inner part

Example   The outside of the car was white, but the **interior** was red.

Respond

What kind of car would you like to have? Would you want a red **interior** or would another color suit you better? Describe how you would like the **interior** of your car to look.

_____

_____

_____

_____

_____

_____

_____

_____

_____

_____

_____

_____

_____

_____

_____

_____

_____

Jaunty

Definition   Stylish; lively or carefree

Example   Bob always wore his hat at a **jaunty** angle.

Respond

Bob, in his **jaunty** hat, and his friend, Jake, walked **jauntily** down the street.
When you read the previous sentence, what kind of picture did you see?
Is it happy or sad, pleasant or unpleasant? Describe what you see when
you read the word **jaunty**.

_____

_____

_____

_____

_____

_____

_____

_____

_____

_____

_____

_____

_____

_____

_____

_____

_____

Jester

Definition   A person whose words or actions cause or are intended to cause amusement or laughter

Example   In medieval times, the court **jester** provided entertainment for royal families.

Respond

In *Hamlet,* one of William Shakespeare's plays, the **jester** Yorick is fondly remembered by the main character. King Henry VIII's **jester**, Will Somers, was also famous. Today's **jesters** no longer perform just for royalty. They are the comics or comedians we see on television and the stage. Name a famous modern-day "**jester**" and explain why he or she is considered funny.

_____

_____

_____

_____

_____

_____

_____

_____

_____

_____

_____

_____

_____

_____

Knack

Definition   A special skill; the power to do something easily

Example   Maria really has a **knack** for using the computer.

Respond

Do you have a **knack** for anything? Maybe it's only for getting in trouble. Someone you know probably has a **knack** for something that others would love to have. What is the **knack** that this person has and why do you think he or she has it?

_____

_____

_____

_____

_____

_____

_____

_____

_____

_____

_____

_____

_____

_____

Linger

Definition To stay on; to be slow to leave

Example "We shouldn't **linger** too long over dinner," said Bunny to Peter. "The children will be worried."

Respond

There is always a temptation to **linger** in a pleasant setting. Have you ever **lingered** too long somewhere and been late getting home? What happened when you got there?

_____

_____

_____

_____

_____

_____

_____

_____

_____

_____

_____

_____

_____

_____

_____

_____

Listless

Definition   Not interested in things; too tired to care

Example   George was very **listless** in school today.

Respond

Attending ball games, movies, and other forms of entertainment on school nights can make students **listless** in school the next day. What are some other reasons why a student might be **listless** in school?

_____

_____

_____

_____

_____

_____

_____

_____

_____

_____

_____

_____

_____

_____

_____

_____

_____

Name _____ Date _____

Lubricate

Definition   To make something smooth or
slippery, such as the parts of
a machine

Example   Joey used a special grease
to **lubricate** the steering on
his tractor.

Respond

What might you need to **lubricate**? What would you use to **lubricate** it?
Explain the process.

_____

_____

_____

_____

_____

_____

_____

_____

_____

_____

_____

_____

_____

_____

49

Mishap

Definition An unlucky accident

Example Luis had a **mishap** on the way to town.

Respond

Flat tires, broken mirrors, spilled milk, and torn clothes are all **mishaps**. Would a serious car accident be considered a **mishap**? Why or why not?

_____

_____

_____

_____

_____

_____

_____

_____

_____

_____

_____

_____

_____

_____

_____

_____

_____

_____

_____

_____

_____

Mistletoe

Definition   A plant with small, shiny green leaves and white berries

Example   **Mistletoe** is traditionally used as a decoration at Christmastime.

Respond

Another tradition is that a person who stands under the **mistletoe** may be kissed. If you could be under the **mistletoe** with any person, living or dead, who would it be and why?

_____

_____

_____

_____

_____

_____

_____

_____

_____

_____

_____

_____

_____

_____

_____

_____

_____

Modest

Definition   Not thinking too highly of oneself; not vain; humble

Example   Greg was very **modest** about his achievements in track-and-field events.

Respond

Many winners are very **modest** about their successes. Do you have a special talent you are **modest** about? What is it and why are you **modest**?

_____

_____

_____

_____

_____

_____

_____

_____

_____

_____

_____

_____

_____

_____

_____

_____

_____

Neglect

Definition To give little attention or respect to

Example If you **neglect** to renew your driver's license, you may get a ticket.

Respond

Jack knew he should have his license renewed, but he just **neglected** to do it. Suddenly he realized that he had **neglected** it too long. His license had expired! What do you think Jack will do now? Will he have learned his lesson about **neglecting** important things?

_____

_____

_____

_____

_____

_____

_____

_____

_____

_____

_____

_____

_____

_____

_____

_____

Nook

Definition   A cozy little corner

Example   Susie likes to curl up in a **nook** to read.

Respond

Do you have a favorite **nook** where you like to go to read or listen to music? Is it "your" spot? What makes this **nook** special?

_____

_____

_____

_____

_____

_____

_____

_____

_____

_____

_____

_____

_____

_____

_____

_____

Novelty

Definition A new or unusual thing
or occurrence

Example The baby became bored with
his toy when the **novelty** wore off.

Respond

Sales skyrocket when a **novelty** appears in the stores. However, sales drop when
the **novelty** of the item wears off. Discuss why this happens and why people are
so eager to own a **novelty**. What **novelties** have you purchased for yourself?

_____

_____

_____

_____

_____

_____

_____

_____

_____

_____

_____

_____

_____

_____

_____

_____

_____

Obsession

Definition A feeling, idea, or impulse that a person cannot escape

Example Marty has an **obsession** with owning his own car.

Respond

Marty can drive the family car whenever he wishes, but that does not suit him. He is totally **obsessed** with having a car of his own. It's all he can talk about. Have you ever been **obsessed** with something? How did you handle it?

_____

_____

_____

_____

_____

_____

_____

_____

_____

_____

_____

_____

_____

_____

Name _____ Date _____

Ominous

Definition   Threatening; unfavorable

Example   There was an **ominous** feeling in
the air on Halloween night.

Respond

Can you think of a time when you had an **ominous** feeling? What did you do?
How did it turn out?

_____

_____

_____

_____

_____

_____

_____

_____

_____

_____

_____

_____

_____

_____

_____

_____

_____

_____

Opponent

Definition   A person who is on the other side in a game or contest

Example   Bart's **opponent** in the final tennis match was his friend Justin.

Respond

Bart and Justin had always been friends, but now they were also **opponents**. Bart wanted desperately to win, and he knew he could, but why did his **opponent** have to be Justin? He knew Justin wanted to win just as badly as he did, and he feared for their friendship, whatever the outcome. Who will win the match and what will the future hold for the two **opponents** and friends?

_____

_____

_____

_____

_____

_____

_____

_____

_____

_____

_____

_____

_____

Panic

Definition   Uncontrolled fear

Example   Jordy felt total **panic** when he
thought he saw a ghost.

Respond

As Jordy raced **panic**-stricken through the house, he was sure the ghost was
right on his heels. What should he do? Where should he go? His **panic** had
led him to believe the ghost was real. How can Jordy solve his problem?

_____

_____

_____

_____

_____

_____

_____

_____

_____

_____

_____

_____

_____

_____

_____

_____

_____

_____

Peeve

Definition   Something that annoys or disturbs

Example   Phillip's pet **peeve** is dirty ashtrays.

Respond

Doesn't everyone have a pet **peeve**? What is yours and why does it **peeve** you? Are others **peeved** by the same thing?

_____

_____

_____

_____

_____

_____

_____

_____

_____

_____

_____

_____

_____

_____

_____

_____

_____

_____

Portion

Definition   A part given to some person; a share

Example   "My **portion** isn't as large as yours,"
Chris said to Dewayne.
   "You got the biggest **portion** last
time," replied Dewayne.

Respond

Portions are shares, but not necessarily equal shares. If you were asked to
divide a pie into **portions** for your family, how would you decide to do it?
Would everyone get an equal **portion**? Why or why not?

_____

_____

_____

_____

_____

_____

_____

_____

_____

_____

_____

_____

_____

_____

_____

_____

_____

Postpone

Definition   To delay

Example   Joe's grades were terrible! He wanted to **postpone** showing his report card to his parents as long as possible.

Respond

Most of us have wanted to **postpone** something in our lives. It might have been showing a bad report card or taking a trip to the dentist. It could have been just doing homework. Does **postponing** something ever make it better, or should we just face it as soon as possible?

_____

_____

_____

_____

_____

_____

_____

_____

_____

_____

_____

_____

_____

_____

_____

Prosperous

Definition   Successful; thriving

Example   Mr. Big was considered the most **prosperous** man in town.

Respond

What do you think of when you think of someone being **prosperous**? Is it fame, money, or a happy life? Who is the most **prosperous** person you know of and why do you consider him or her to be **prosperous**?

_____

_____

_____

_____

_____

_____

_____

_____

_____

_____

_____

_____

_____

_____

_____

_____

Psychology

Definition The science of the human mind and human behavior

Example **Psychology** is studied in order to better understand people's actions, thoughts, feelings, and emotions.

Respond

Do you ever wonder why you feel or act as you do? Studying **psychology** might give you some answers. If you're interested in the behavior of others, you might want to become a **psychologist**. If you decided to study **psychology**, which area of behavior would you be most interested in and why?

_____

_____

_____

_____

_____

_____

_____

_____

_____

_____

_____

_____

_____

_____

Quench

Definition   To satisfy; to put out

Example   Miguel wandered through the desert searching for water to **quench** his thirst.

Respond

Not only do we **quench** our thirst, but we might also **quench** a fire. If you saw a spark from the fireplace begin to burn the carpet, how would you **quench** it?

_____

_____

_____

_____

_____

_____

_____

_____

_____

_____

_____

_____

_____

_____

_____

_____

_____

_____

Recall

Definition   To remember

Example   Kyle wanted to wear his red
sweater to the ball game, but
he couldn't **recall** where he
had left it and his friends
were waiting for him.

Respond

Should Kyle spend time trying to **recall** where he left his sweater or should he
just wear another one? Is it fair to keep your friends waiting while you try to
recall something?

_____

_____

_____

_____

_____

_____

_____

_____

_____

_____

_____

_____

_____

_____

Remote

Definition   Far away; distant

Example   Rashid lived in a **remote** part of the desert.

Respond

What is the most **remote** place you can think of to live?
Would you like to live there? Why or why not?

_____

_____

_____

_____

_____

_____

_____

_____

_____

_____

_____

_____

_____

_____

_____

_____

_____

_____

Rouse

Definition   To wake up

Example   Once upon a time there were two cats named Bosco and Pickles. Bosco wanted to play, but Pickles was sleeping so soundly that Bosco couldn't **rouse** him.

Respond

Have you ever tried to **rouse** someone who was sleeping? Does your mother have trouble **rousing** you for school each morning? What should she do when she can't **rouse** you?

_____

_____

_____

_____

_____

_____

_____

_____

_____

_____

_____

_____

_____

_____

_____

_____

Sanitary

Definition   Free of germs; clean

Example   A hospital must be kept totally **sanitary**.

Respond

Sanitation is very important for a healthy life. Garbage placed in proper containers, correct sewage disposal, and control of air pollution all contribute to a **sanitary** lifestyle. What can you and your classmates do to help keep your school **sanitary**?

_____

_____

_____

_____

_____

_____

_____

_____

_____

_____

_____

_____

_____

_____

_____

Sarcasm

Definition   A sneering or cutting remark

Example   "How graceful you are!" said Ann in
sarcasm as Gail tripped over the chair.

Respond

Sometimes people use **sarcasm** because they are feeling defensive.
Others just have what is often referred to as a **sarcastic** nature.
Do you believe that anyone really has a **sarcastic** nature?
Explain why or why not.

_____

_____

_____

_____

_____

_____

_____

_____

_____

_____

_____

_____

_____

_____

_____

_____

Stress

Definition   Great pressure or force; strain

Example   Mary was feeling the **stress** of finishing her book on time.

Respond

Today's fast-paced lifestyle places **stress** on each of us. Have you heard people say, "I'm completely **stressed** out"? What puts **stress** on you? What can you do to relieve this **stress**?

_____

_____

_____

_____

_____

_____

_____

_____

_____

_____

_____

_____

_____

_____

_____

_____

_____

Superstition

Definition   A belief or practice resulting from fear of the unknown, trust in magic or chance, or a false idea of cause

Example   A long-standing **superstition** is that any time the 13th of the month falls on a Friday, it will be an unlucky day.

Respond

Other common bad-luck **superstitions** include walking under a ladder or having a black cat cross your path. Some people have their own personal **superstitions**, such as believing that a certain item of clothing is lucky. If you or someone you know has a special **superstition**, tell about it.

_____

_____

_____

_____

_____

_____

_____

_____

_____

_____

_____

Subscribe

Definition   To promise to take and pay for a number of copies of a newspaper or magazine

Example   Jamal's family plans to **subscribe** to the local newspaper.

Respond

The sale of magazine **subscriptions** is often used as a money-raising project for a school. Does your family **subscribe** to any magazines or newspapers? Do you **subscribe** to anything just for yourself?

_____

_____

_____

_____

_____

_____

_____

_____

_____

_____

_____

_____

_____

_____

_____

_____

_____

_____

Suburb

Definition   A town near a large city

Example   Madison is a **suburb** of Nashville.

Respond

Nashville, known as Music City, USA, has many **suburban** areas. Living in the **suburbs**, gives access to all the advantages of city life while being able to avoid the hustle and bustle of the city. Would you prefer to live in the city or the **suburbs**? Why?

_____

_____

_____

_____

_____

_____

_____

_____

_____

_____

_____

_____

_____

_____

_____

_____

Thigh

Definition   The part of the leg between
the hip and the knee

Example   The football team did daily
exercises to strengthen their
thigh muscles.

Respond

Strong **thigh** muscles are an important asset for any football player.
If you were a football player, would exercising your **thigh** muscles
be a priority for you? Why or why not?

_____

_____

_____

_____

_____

_____

_____

_____

_____

_____

_____

_____

_____

_____

_____

_____

Triumphant

Definition   Rejoicing because of victory or success

Example   The University of Kentucky Wildcats were **triumphant** after winning the 1996 NCAA championship.

Respond

It's March 2010. Kentucky is again one of the final four. Who will win the NCAA tournament this year? Will UK be **triumphant** again?

_____

_____

_____

_____

_____

_____

_____

_____

_____

_____

_____

_____

_____

_____

_____

_____

Twilight

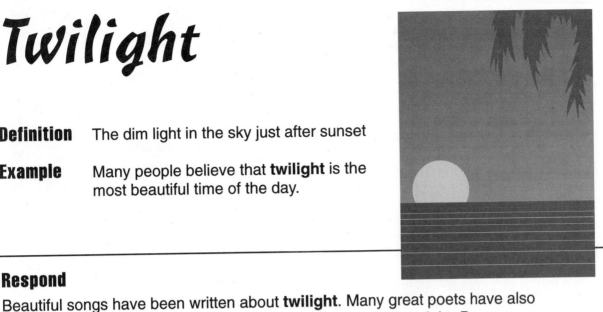

Definition   The dim light in the sky just after sunset

Example   Many people believe that **twilight** is the most beautiful time of the day.

Respond

Beautiful songs have been written about **twilight**. Many great poets have also written about **twilight**, some referring to it as the door to the night. Do you like the **twilight**? What is your favorite time of the day and why?

_____

_____

_____

_____

_____

_____

_____

_____

_____

_____

_____

_____

_____

_____

_____

_____

Undertake

Definition   To set about; to attempt

Example   Tawana is about to **undertake** the biggest task of her career.

Respond

Is it a major promotion? An important report? No, Tawana is going to **undertake** fixing the office copier. If she doesn't **undertake** the job, no one else will and she can't finish her work. Have you ever been in a situation like this? How did you solve your problem?

_____

_____

_____

_____

_____

_____

_____

_____

_____

_____

_____

_____

_____

_____

_____

_____

_____

Unique

Definition   Having no like or equal; one of a kind

Example   The Statue of Liberty is a **unique** landmark.

Respond

Have you ever heard *someone* described as **unique**?
Think of a **unique** person. Why is he or she **unique**?

_____

_____

_____

_____

_____

_____

_____

_____

_____

_____

_____

_____

_____

_____

_____

_____

_____

_____

Vacate

Definition   To leave a place empty

Example   The family was asked to **vacate** their home because of a gas leak.

Respond

Have you ever had to **vacate** your home? What are some other reasons one might find it necessary to **vacate** a building?

_____

_____

_____

_____

_____

_____

_____

_____

_____

_____

_____

_____

_____

_____

_____

_____

_____

Variable

Definition   Changeable

Example   The weather forecaster predicted **variable** winds for today.

Respond

Just as the winds are **variable**, people may be also. Some are friendly one day and don't know you the next. You probably know someone like that. Do these actions bother you, and if so, how do you handle it?

_____

_____

_____

_____

_____

_____

_____

_____

_____

_____

_____

_____

_____

_____

_____

Name _____ Date _____

Venison

Definition   The meat of a deer

Example   Juan looked forward to eating
venison during hunting season.

Respond

During colonial days **venison** was a very important food. Someone in each
family went hunting whenever meat was needed. Can you imagine living like that
today? Plan a meal you would like with **venison** as the main dish.

_____

_____

_____

_____

_____

_____

_____

_____

_____

_____

_____

_____

_____

_____

_____

_____

_____

Version

Definition   A description or report told from one person's point of view

Example   You could have heard a pin drop in the courtroom as the prosecution presented their **version** of the case. However, when the defense told their **version**, people clapped their hands, shouted, and stamped their feet.

Respond

In court, everyone has the right to tell his or her **version** of a situation. How might the different reactions to two **versions** affect the outcome of a case?

_____

_____

_____

_____

_____

_____

_____

_____

_____

_____

_____

_____

_____

_____

_____

Name _____ Date _____

Void

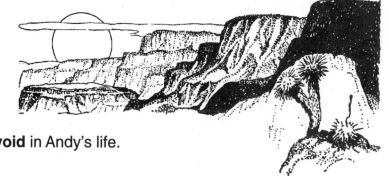

Definition   An empty space

Example   Darla's leaving left a **void** in Andy's life.

Respond

Have you had an experience that left a **void** in your life? Was it a small **void** or a big empty hole? What did you do to try to fill the **void**? Tell the story.

_____

_____

_____

_____

_____

_____

_____

_____

_____

_____

_____

_____

_____

_____

_____

_____

_____

_____

_____

Wander

Definition   To move about without a fixed course, aim, or goal

Example   Do you **wander** in the mall every Saturday?

Respond

There are many people who spend much of their time just **wandering** around. Arnie is a good example of a **wanderer**. When asked why he just **wandered** all the time, he replied, "I have nothing else to do." Place yourself in Arnie's position and make a plan to stop spending so much time **wandering**.

_____

_____

_____

_____

_____

_____

_____

_____

_____

_____

_____

_____

_____

_____

_____

_____

Wheedle

Definition   To persuade by using soft words or flattery

Example   Judy knows that her Mom probably won't want to buy her an expensive new watch for her birthday, so she decides to try to **wheedle** it from her.

Respond

"Mom, you sure look pretty today," Judy says. "And isn't that a new dress you're wearing? I really like it." Almost everyone uses **wheedling** at some time. Have you ever **wheedled** to get something you wanted? How did it turn out?

_____

_____

_____

_____

_____

_____

_____

_____

_____

_____

_____

_____

_____

_____

_____

Yearn

Definition   To have a strong desire for something

Example   Do you ever **yearn** for things that appear to be beyond your reach?

Respond

What do you **yearn** for? Fame, wealth, beauty, health, happiness? What do you think will be the outcome of your **yearning**?

_____

_____

_____

_____

_____

_____

_____

_____

_____

_____

_____

_____

_____

_____

_____

_____

_____

_____

Youngster

Definition   A young person; a child or youth

Example   When Carlos was a **youngster**, he had a newspaper route.

Respond

As a **youngster** you may have a part-time job or certain chores to do at home. Should all **youngsters** have responsibilities? Give your opinions and tell why you feel this way.

_____

_____

_____

_____

_____

_____

_____

_____

_____

_____

_____

_____

_____

_____

_____

_____

_____

_____

Zone

Definition An area that is set apart for some special purpose

Example As Marsha parked her car in the handicapped parking **zone** and dashed into the grocery store for a quart of milk, she never dreamed that her car would be gone when she returned.

Respond

Why was Marsha's car gone when she returned? What is a "handicapped parking **zone**"? Can you think of any other kinds of **zones**?

_____

_____

_____

_____

_____

_____

_____

_____

_____

_____

_____

_____

_____

_____

Zoology

Definition The science that deals with animals and animal life

Example Henry took **zoology** classes in college because he planned to be a zookeeper.

Respond

You have just been appointed zookeeper for the new zoo in your hometown. You will be given the money to pay for the first ten animals, and the choice will be yours. Will **zoology** classes be of help to you in making your choices? Which ten animals will you choose?

_____

_____

_____

_____

_____

_____

_____

_____

_____

_____

_____

_____

_____

_____